Finding and
following
God's calling in your
vocation

So what am I gonna do with my LIFE?

Finding and
following
God's calling in your
vocation

[So what am I gonna do with my LIFE?]

Diane Lindsey
Reeves

Youth Specialties

ZondervanPublishingHouse
Grand Rapids, Michigan

A Division of HarperCollinsPublishers

So What Am I Gonna Do with My Life? Journaling Workbook for Students: Finding and following God's calling in your vocation

Youth Specialties Books, 300 S. Pierce St., El Cajon, CA 92020, are published by Zondervan Publishing House, 5300 Patterson, S.E., Grand Rapids, MI 49530.

ISBN 0-310-23374-7

Edited by Tamara Rice
Cover and interior design by DesignPoint, Inc.

Printed in the United States of America

01 02 03 04 05 06 07 / / 10 9 8 7 6 5 4 3 2 1

CONTENTS

How to USE this book

So what *are* you gonna do with your life? Get by on charm and looks? Hang out at your parents' house till they throw you out? Go away to college and party the next four years away? Get a job and lurk around trying to find yourself?

Good luck! Maybe you'd rather try—

- Something a little more daring
- Something a little more original
- Something that will make you think and laugh and cry
- Something that will make you crazy with frustration and wild with anticipation
- Something that will satisfy and challenge—and make your mama proud!

Maybe you'd like to...

GET A LIFE!

If so, this book is for you. It's your chance to dream big dreams, try new ideas, and get in touch with the one who has your best interests at heart—God. It's your place to think through tough questions, connect with people who have answers, and get yourself used to living *on* purpose, *with* purpose, and *for* a purpose.

This book is about your future. It's about your chance to do all you were meant to do and be all you were meant to be.

Use this book to—

- Discover God's big plans for your life
- Seek answers about your future
- Make the most of every God-given ability and opportunity
- Allow others to invest in your life
- Commit to give life all you've got

It won't be easy. It won't happen overnight. But it will be worth it.

This journal is your tool. Use it to think through one of the biggest choices you'll ever make: what to do with your life. The first four sections include opportunities to—

- Take a good long look at who you are and what you want out of life
- Uncover Scripture's timeless principles about success
- Build confidence as you take to heart God's promises about your future
- Reach out to others for support, advice, and ideas
- Pursue a life fully committed to God

The focus of the first three sections is on discovering what—by God's grace—you have to offer the world, while the focus of the last section is on finding what the world has to offer you. And of course, the ultimate goal is to put the two together into a perfect match. Find your place in the world of work—where you can take a stand, make a difference, and earn a living.

The After Hours section will introduce some nuts-and-bolts skills you can use for a lifetime of workplace success. These activities will get you—

- Looking beyond the obvious
- Taking advantage of technology and other resources to find the best options
- Making informed decisions about your future

The best advice for getting the most from this journal is summed up in this old saying:

Pray as though everything depended on God; work as though everything depended on you.

[To Be or Not to Be]

Remember when you were a kid and grownups would smile funny and ask you, "What do you want to be when you grow up?" What did you say? Write it here.

What would you say if someone asked you that question now? What *do* you want to be when you grow up? Really and truly. Deep down in your heart. Even if your idea sounds weird or impossible. Write it here.

Don't laugh. Researchers are finding evidence that these very first inklings often prove to be the best ideas about the kind of work that's best for you. Spontaneous ideas that are pure—unadulterated by pessimism or doubt. Ideas that bloom before well-meaning people or life's circumstances convince you you're nuts to even think you could do something like that.

Think of these ideas as rough, unpolished diamonds. Neither of the ideas you wrote above may prove to be the one and only thing you were meant to do on earth. But they might hold some valuable clues for planning your future career.

For instance, what do these ideas say about you? What do these ideas say about your attitude toward work or what you want out of life? Maybe these ideas show a gravitation toward money or fame. Or maybe you want your life to make a difference. Maybe you want to work with your hands. Perhaps you have creative ideas that need to be expressed. What is it that pulls you toward the ideas you wrote above?

Hold on to those thoughts and keep moving through the activities that follow.

[First Impressions]

Ever heard the saying, "First impressions are lasting impressions"? Well, it's true. Prove it by completing the following statements with the first thought that pops into your head. Don't stop to psychoanalyze your answers, just write down your first idea.

- The thing I most want out of life is—

- When I think of my future, I—

- People often tell me I'm good at—

- Sometimes I feel as if God were leading me to—

- The most important accomplishment of my life so far is—

- It's not really important that I—

- Whatever it takes, I'm determined to—

> ## It's a Gift!
> As God's children, we're blessed with many gifts. Some gifts or abilities are with us from the day we're born (Psalm 139:13-16). Others are given when we become Christians (1 Corinthians 12:4-7). Still others come just in time, when God has a job for us to do—as was the case for Bezalel in Exodus 31. What talents and abilities have *you* been blessed with so far?

Now that you've captured your first reactions, go back and give these statements some thought. As you look at each, ask yourself *why*. Think about it. Pray about it. And be honest with yourself. These questions are some of the most important for you to answer. Oddly enough, some people go their entire lives without answering them. Don't be one of those people!

[Pile It On!]

What if choosing your life's work was like making your favorite sandwich? A little of this, a lot of that, hold the pickles…and you've got it made. Well, if it were like making a sandwich, which of the following ingredients would you want to include in your ideal work situation? Go ahead, pick all that apply!

People

Babies

Children

Teenagers

Men

Women

People with special needs

Elderly people

Other _____

Motivation

Helping others

Serving God

Discovering new things

Making a difference

Making money

Being famous

Having fun

Other _____

Tools

Technology

Machines

Trucks and heavy equipment

Animals

Plants

Food

Medicine

Other _____

Places

Big city

Small town

Rural community

Foreign country

Store

Office

On the water

In the air

Outdoors

Other _____

Ideas

Written words

Spoken words

Numbers

Problems and solutions

Artistic creations

Other _____

[Everybody Has a Story]

Don't look now, but you're surrounded. Surrounded by people who can help you figure out what to do with your life. They may be strangers. They may be people you've always wanted to meet. They may be friends or neighbors. They may even be—gulp!—your very own parents. They've all been in your shoes, faced the tough decisions, and learned some hard lessons. Truth is, they all have a story to tell about their experiences with work, and what they've learned can help you in a big way.

So get them talking!

An informal (and nonexistent) survey of American adults has shown 99.9 percent of all working and retired people are happy to tell you about their work life—if you'll just ask. (CIA agents can't talk about their work.)

Get the inside story from a parent, grandparent, or other relative; from someone you admire like a coach, youth leader, or teacher; or from someone with a job you think you might like—whether you know them personally or not. Before you embark on this enlightening interview, check out the suggestions below.

RALLY WITH WORDS

A good interview is like a game of tennis. You lob a question; they return the answer. Back and forth; back and forth. Keep your eye on the ball and return each serve with precision.

When interviewing someone, have several questions in mind but always think on your feet to dig deeper into interesting ideas that surface during the course of conversation. Follow up and get all the details. Keep notes and use the space on page 13 to record what you find out.

Here are a few suggested questions to get you started. Add some of your own.

- What was your very first job like?
- What do you do now?
- How did you get into this field?
- What do you like most about it?
- What do you like least about it?
- What would you do differently if you had it to do all over again?

[*Come Again?*
For posterity's sake or to free you to focus your attention on your interviewee, record or videotape your conversations in addition to jotting down notes. A good conversation with a parent, grandparent, or some other special person could well become a treasured memory.]

[Life Story]

Featuring—

Date—

What my friend said—

What I've learned—

Brownie Points

A thank-you note is always a good idea when someone has taken the time to help you out. It's not only a nice thing to do, but you just never know where it might lead. To find out how a simple note set off a chain of events that spanned several decades and led all the way to the White House, read Chad Foster's book *Teenagers: Preparing for the Real World* (Rising Books, 1995).

The Word on Work

Nowhere—not even on the *New York Times* bestseller list—will you find better advice about success than in the book of Proverbs. Written by King Solomon—one of the all-time richest and smartest guys—it's the most profound how-to-succeed manual, bar none. See what this wise guy had to say about work in some of the following verses:

Verses	Key idea
Proverbs 10:4	[ ]
Proverbs 12:11	[ ]
Proverbs 12:24	[ ]
Proverbs 13:4	[ ]
Proverbs 13:11-12	[ ]
Proverbs 13:19	[ ]
Proverbs 21:5	[ ]
Proverbs 22:29	[ ]

So now that you've read King Solomon's how-to manual for success, what did you find out?

- What results can you expect if you work hard?

- What traits are common in successful workers?

- What part do goals and desires play in finding success?

- What about taking action and learning new skills?

Now about laziness… a word to the wise.

Lazy people want much but get little, but those who work hard will prosper and be satisfied.

—*Proverbs 13:4*

Christians at Work

ANGELA ELWELL HUNT

author

If someone had told Angela Elwell Hunt 20 years ago she would someday be the author of 76 books (and the number continues to grow), she would have thought the person was crazy—absolutely, positively, certifiably crazy. Angie says she never dreamed of becoming a writer—though she does admit to writing "God wants me to become a poem writer" in her fifth-grade journal at summer camp.

But for years, her destiny seemed to be in music. She initially pursued a music degree in college and even traveled the world in a Christian singing group. But one thing kept coming up—*words*. She liked them, and they liked her. Using them well came naturally. Although it took a while to get the hint, Angie says God used other people to nudge her in the right direction.

That nudging started in a blizzard while Angie was on the road giving concerts with the singing group. When the group was stranded for four days, the leader asked team members to keep journals recording their impressions of the experience. When he read what Angie had written he encouraged her to think about putting her way with words to work.

Shortly thereafter Angie changed her college major to English literature and started her career as a high school English teacher. But it didn't take long to figure out teaching wasn't something she wanted to do for the rest of her life—no offense, students. So she went on to help write curriculum for a church youth department and later to work as a secretary for a well-known newspaper columnist. Though these professions weren't necessarily Angela's dream jobs, each experience built her skills and confidence as a writer.

It all paid off when she went out on her own and started working as a freelance writer composing letters, brochures, and advertising copy for businesses and magazines. Reading books and learning from mistakes were her two best teachers during the five years she devoted to this pursuit.

In 1988, Angie took the plunge. She wrote a children's picture book and entered it in a contest for unpublished children's book authors. It was one of 500 entries. And it won! With a story called *If I Had Long, Long Hair* (now out of print), Angie's career as an author was officially launched.

Her early prayer, "Please, God, let me get published," has been replaced—with God's help—by a heartfelt desire to write a book that will endure. Some say she's already written it in *The Tale of Three Trees* (Chariot Victor Publications, 1989). Angie describes it as a simple story about three trees who got everything they wanted but nothing they had asked for.

Maybe that's the story that will endure, or maybe not. But it doesn't stop Angie from pouring her heart into every book she writes. Always trying new genres, she has written books for children, teenagers, and adults—some fiction, some nonfiction.

Angie believes her writing is a gift much like the talents the master gave his servants in Matthew 25. Her take is that God may give us talents, but we've got to do the work to use them. When it comes to sharing her talent with the world, Angie's creed is "Use it or lose it."

[
To find out more about Angie's work, visit her Web site at www.angelaelwellhunt.com.
]

[Holy Résumés]

So you're not part of the in-crowd? Not a sports hero? Can't sing? Can't dance? The only tune you play is the latest CD? Struggling to get decent grades? And no one's begging to have your picture on a magazine cover either?

Might as well throw in the towel and resign yourself to life as a loser, huh?

Hey, wait a sec! When God's reading résumés, you can rest assured *rich*, *beautiful*, and *popular* aren't on his list of high-in-demand skills. Remember, you're dealing with the guy who's famous for things like making the last into the first and the least into the greatest. If he's got a job for you to do, he'll give you all the right stuff to do it—no matter what anyone else says or thinks, no matter how it looks today, and no matter how things are *supposed* to be.

If you don't believe it, just look at some of the people he hired for some of the biggest jobs in history.

MOSES

It was nothing but excuses when God called Moses to lead his people to the Promised Land. Find out if God bought any of Moses' lame excuses in Exodus 3:13-4:17.

What excuses are *you* making? How do God's responses to Moses apply to you today?

Your excuses—

God's responses—

ESTHER

She was just a woman—which in those days meant she had no power, no clout, and no authority. But timing is everything in a story like Esther's. Read Esther 4:7-16 to find out how a queen found her destiny by risking her life.

How might God want to use *you* to further his kingdom? Look back again at verse 14.

RAHAB

Bad, bad girl is all you can say about Rahab's choice of professions. Not exactly a goody-two-shoes, yet she was the one God used to save an entire nation. See for yourself in Joshua 2:1-24. Who says you have to be perfect to be used by God? Rahab is proof that perfection isn't what God is looking for.

What areas in your life keep you from feeling worthy of being used by God?

PETER

Ah, Peter! Impulsive, pushy, and so doggone inquisitive—always testing the limits. Jumping out of boats without the faith to stay afloat (Matthew 14:22-32), cutting off people's ears (John 18:1-11)— actually it was just one person's ear, but still.

Let's face it, the guy could be a pain. But give Peter a couple years of hanging out with Jesus, and he was slowly transformed—flaws and all. Even Jesus called him the rock on which he would build the church (Matthew 16:17-19).

Read about Peter.

Do *you* need to confess any Peter-like behavior in your own life? Ask God to make a difference in your heart and mold you into his image. Take heart—if God can change Peter, he can change you!

When God went looking for a king, he passed over the great and went for a nobody: David—a mere kid who looked after his father's sheep. But he was a kid who loved the Lord with all his heart and was handpicked by God to become one of the greatest leaders who ever lived. Read 1 Samuel 16:1-13.

Is your heart ready for God's call? Let God do great things with your life. Use the space below to record your prayer.

Pick a Favorite

What other Bible stories can you think of in which God made the weak strong, the foolish wise, and otherwise made big things happen in little lives? Pick a favorite and describe what happens here.

[Mirror, Mirror on the Wall]

Some people go about this career thing all wrong. They bust their chops getting good grades, they haul their heinies off to college, and then they end up taking any job that comes along just to get a paycheck. Day after day they drag themselves off to a job they can't stand—all in the name of responsibility.

So what's wrong with that system?

Nothing, until you realize who does the time—some 86,000 hours of it. That's how much time the average person spends on the job during a lifetime. (It's a long time!) Kind of makes all those years in school seem like a walk in the park, doesn't it?

So here's the question: *Do you really want to get stuck doing something you don't want to do?*

At its best, work is a fulfilling way to spend your days, a means of expressing all you are, and a way of giving to the world. At its worst? Well, it's just work. But there's a big difference between the two.

Know thyself—these two immortal words explain the secret passageway between enduring a job and enjoying a career. You've got to know *who* you are, *what* you like, and what you *want* out of life before you can really decide how to spend all that time with gusto. You were created on purpose and by design, so it's important to find out just what makes you *you*. Here's a simple exercise to get you started.

Describe yourself in 10 words or less.

List three ways you like to spend your time.

1.

2.

3.

List three things guaranteed to bore you to tears.

1.

2.

3.

Recall two good things people have said about you.

1.

2.

List the one thing you like best about yourself.

List the one thing you like least about yourself.

Now use as many words as you need to paint a colorful picture of your dream job.

[RIP]

Still trying to figure out how to start your life as an adult? Try a little reverse psychology. Imagine that instead of standing on the brink of your entire future, you're sitting in a rocking chair at the end of a well-lived life.

Looking back, what would you want your life to have counted for? What accomplishments would you be most proud of? How would you want to be remembered?

Use these insights to get your life started on the right track.

[Satisfaction Guaranteed]

Never. No way.

Is that how likely it seems for your hopes and dreams to come true? Especially now that you've looked in the mirror, and there isn't an incredibly exceptional person looking back?

Not yet anyway.

Think of yourself as a work in progress, under construction. God won't leave you high and dry—that's a promise.

Look up Philippians 1:6 and write it, word for word, in the space below.

Now write it on your heart (*memorize* it!) so you'll remember it always. It's a *promise*, God's ironclad guarantee. He's there for you…for the long haul.

[Dropping Hints]

Here's an activity that's sure to get you blushing. Ask 10 people who know you fairly well, "What's the best thing about me?" Well, maybe you should preface the question with a little explanation about how you're doing some thinking about what future career would be good for you, and as part of the process you'd like feedback from others who know you well—and you've selected him or her! And here are two guidelines for them: (1) It has to be something good, and (2) it can't be about how you look. You're looking for your best trait or something you do especially well.

Then, ask away—and *listen* to the answer! Even jot notes in the space provided.

No need to feel like you're fishing for compliments. No reason to feel shy. (But if you just can't bring yourself to ask, why not have a friend or family member ask for you and give you the results?)

The benefit of this activity is insight into areas you may never have noticed before.

List 10 people here.

What's the best thing about me? Write the answers below.

[Christians at Work]

ANNA QUAN
physician

Is Dr. Anna Quan a physician who happens to be a Christian or a Christian who happens to be a physician? Anna prefers to think of herself as the latter—a Christian first and a doctor second.

Back in high school Anna was one of those students who excelled in every subject—a self-admitted nerd. She had lots of interests at that time, but during her senior year Anna's interests narrowed a little. She got a close look at the medical profession when her best friend suffered a major illness that lingered over several months. Anna spent a lot of time visiting her friend at the hospital and noticed the impact doctors had on their patients' lives and health. A doctor's bedside manner could literally make or break a patient's day.

Suddenly Anna's eyes were opened and she began to see full-time medical work as a great way to minister to others, a way that she could merge her knack for science and her desire to work with people.

But first there was a lot of learning to be done and a lot of decisions to be made. When choosing which college to attend, Anna and her parents visited two schools that were close to her family's home. The first school was all wrong for her, and she knew it instinctively. But as they walked around the second—Stanford University—Anna says it seemed like there was music in the air. Both Anna and her parents left the campus knowing it was the place for her.

And they were right. Anna says she never felt what she thought of as a clear "calling" toward medicine—there was no neon sign dangling from heaven—but Anna experienced peace when she enrolled in the pre-med program at Stanford. Every time she took a course, she liked it better than the one before and felt that this natural affinity with the medical curriculum confirmed the way God was leading her.

Now after many years of training, Anna specializes in internal medicine and works at a hospital for veterans, where she wrestles with the day-to-day challenges of living her faith in an important and demanding field. She spends most of her time treating older patients with serious illnesses. Anna prays for opportunities to comfort and exhort her patients and asks God for compassion to understand her patients' needs and experiences.

But as much as she loves her work, Anna knows it doesn't define her. If she stopped working tomorrow, she'd still be the same person—wife, mother, doctor—but first of all and most of all, Anna defines herself as a Christian.

[Fact or Fiction]

As if it weren't already hard enough to figure out what to do with your life, you also have to deal with weird ideas that may lead you down the wrong paths. So it's a good idea to test your knowledge of what you can expect when it comes to finding God's will for your life. Mark each statement with F for false.

_____ 1. When God wants you to know his will for your life, he'll have the plan delivered to you in a special-delivery envelope by a messenger on a scooter.

_____ 2. Figuring out God's will is a one-shot deal—figure it out now and you'll have it made for a lifetime.

_____ 3. There's only one way to get to where God wants you—if you miss the turn, you've missed the right road for good.

_____ 4. If you're a good Christian, you'll make serving God your full-time career—minister, youth pastor, missionary, Sunday school teacher—it doesn't matter as long as you're working in full-time ministry.

_____ 5. Find God's will and you're guaranteed to be a success. The road you travel will be smooth all the way.

Ready or not, here come the answers...

1. *False.* Although God sometimes has a flair for the dramatic—burning bushes, blinding lights, and strange dreams—these days he works in more subtle ways, through the truths revealed in his Word, the godly counsel of others, the open doors of opportunity, and that nagging desire that just won't go away. You've got to listen and you've got to seek. And sometimes you need to wait patiently.

2. *Afraid not.* God operates on a need-to-know basis—you'll find your way bit by bit. If you knew the whole story now, you'd never believe it and you might be overwhelmed. Every job prepares you for the future. In the future, when you're sitting in a rocker with a blanket on your lap, you'll be able to look back over your life and see how all the pieces fit together.

3. *No again.* Good thing for you God's an equal opportunity employer. Whatever it takes, no matter how many detours you take along the way, he'll get you there eventually. Mind you, it may take a while—just ask Sarah (Genesis 18:1-15).

4. *Thank goodness, it's false.* In case you haven't noticed, God likes variety. Look at nature—leaves, flowers, bugs, snowflakes—variety is everywhere. So what makes you think he would get tunnel vision when it comes to people? From preacher to plumber, "whatever your hand finds to do, do it with all your might" (Ecclesiastes 9:10).

5. *Shucks! It just doesn't work that way.* You've got to pay your dues—no matter who you are. Joseph started as a slave and ended up a prisoner before he rose through the ranks to become second in command of Egypt. Read the story of his climb in Genesis 37-48 (one of the most gripping stories in the Bible).

Most success stories—no matter how glitzy or glamorous—are the result of years of hard work and preparation. Good thing getting there is half the fun, huh?

[Heart Attack]

Time and time again Scripture records the most unlikely success stories. Ordinary people used in extraordinary ways. The common ingredient of their success? Hearts full of faith. Hearts fully committed to being used by God.

God was able to use these seemingly little people in big ways because their hearts were right with him. Read Paul's roll call of the faithful in Hebrews 11. Note the heroes Paul lists along with their heroic deeds.

Heroes   *Acts of Faith*

What about you? Are you ready for the work God has for you to do? Use these verses to give yourself a spiritual checkup and to note the symptoms of a healthy heart attitude.

Verses   Symptoms of a Healthy Heart Attitude

Joshua 24:15   [   ]

1 Chronicles 28:9   [   ]

Psalm 51:10-12   [   ]

Psalm 139:23   [   ]

Proverbs 4:23   [   ]

Proverbs 16:9   [   ]

Proverbs 21:2   [   ]

Rx

See any symptoms of trouble in your life? Write them here. According to the verses you've just read, what's the cure? Try a good dose of prayer and let God use his healing touch on your heart.

[Live and Learn]

Good decisions. Bad decisions. People everywhere make their share of both. You can learn from your own choices and from those of others.

It's a good idea to talk to people who have already been in your shoes. People who've made the big choices and have lived long enough to see the results. People like your parents, your grandparents, and other trusted adults. Find out what the years of living with their decisions have taught them. Listen and learn.

Use the following three questions to learn important lessons from three people who are important to you.

Name—

When you were my age, what did you want to do with your life?

Why did you—or didn't you—do it?

What would you do differently?

Name—

When you were my age, what did you want to do with your life?

Why did you—or didn't you—do it?

What would you do differently?

Name—

When you were my age, what did you want to do with your life?

Why did you—or didn't you—do it?

What would you do differently?

[In God We Trust]

Can you trust God with your future? How has he done with your life so far? Take a few minutes to make a list of all the ways God has proven himself trustworthy in your life. Include answered prayers and evidence of his presence, provision, and protection in your life.

You know there are really only two things you can count on in your future:

- Jesus Christ
- Change

The rest of your life will be marked by constant change. You can count on it. But you can also count on this: "Jesus Christ is the same yesterday and today and forever" (Hebrews 13:8). Yes!

Christians at Work

JOE MARKHAM

founder and president of Kong Company

Once upon a time there was a dog named Fritz, a guy named Joe, and a Volkswagen van.

Fritz, retired from a police canine unit, had one very annoying habit—he liked to chew on rocks. His owner—Joe—loved Fritz but wasn't crazy about the idea of a dog with no teeth, which is how Fritz would end up if he didn't stop chewing rocks.

One day while Joe was working on his Volkswagen van, Fritz was doing the usual rock chomp. Desperate to get Fritz to stop, Joe starting tossing car parts to him to divert his attention. Nothing worked until Joe pulled off a suspension part and tossed it to Fritz. It was bouncy. It was tough. And it was love at first bite for Fritz.

It was also the inspiration Joe needed to see big dollar signs in his future.

At that point in his life, making money was important to Joe. The prospect of making lots of it was all he needed to drop everything and set up a shop in his basement. He set out to refine his invention and start the business to sell it. He admits making big bucks was his primary motivation in the early years, but making money was not to be…at least not in the beginning.

For one thing Joe had a serious substance abuse problem. And for another, as soon as Joe's product hit the streets, a big competitor knocked it off. They copied Joe's product right down to the packaging design. Of course Joe wasn't too happy about that and took them to court.

He poured nearly every penny he had into a legal battle against the "bad guys." But for reasons he still doesn't understand, the bad guys won.

And then everything was gone: his business, his money, his dream. He was at Ground Zero. But it was just the place he needed to be to find a Savior. Joe says it was a new beginning from the moment he put his faith in God. The substance abuse, the greed—they were gone. In their place was immediate evidence God was in control. Almost overnight Joe was offered the best job he'd ever had. It felt like a second chance at life.

Joe worked as director of admissions for an aircraft mechanic training school. He stayed for a couple of years, but the dream of building his own dog toy company wouldn't go away. Now his motivation was different. He didn't want to make a fortune; he wanted to build a company that would honor God.

So he did. He built Kong Company. The new Joe puts people in front of profits. He hires people with special needs to package his products, even though there are cheaper ways he could get the job done. He also provides steady work to stay-at-home mothers who home-school their children, because he believes in what they're doing. Prayer meetings are as likely in the offices of Kong Company as staff meetings. It's simply a good place to work.

The irony is when Joe quit *focusing* on making money, then his business started making money. Kong now sells millions of dog toys all over the world every year.

Joe says it's amazing what happens when you give everything to God.

[To find out more about Joe's company, visit his Web site at www.kongcompany.com.]

[On with the Show!]

So far this process has been an inside job: looking at yourself and your relationship with God and figuring out how your faith and your future connect. Now turn the focus toward the outside: involving others in your hunt for the right track, checking out options, sorting through choices, and still trying to fit the pieces of this all-important puzzle together.

[Way to Go!]

If you're like the average American teen, your life has followed a familiar path so far: school, extracurricular activities, sports, a part-time job or two, and more school.

Get that diploma though, and boy, life does change. The choices are awesome—mind-boggling too. Deciding where you want to go is just the first step—figuring out how you're going to get there can be a doozy.

Just for fun, pick a goal. Something you think you might want to do with your life. Something like a media relations specialist or a tool repairman or graphic designer. Write that goal here.

With that goal in mind, think through the pros and cons of the following post-high school options. Put a check in the last column by any options that help *you* head in the right direction.

Community college or trade school (one to two years of intense technical training for a specific profession)

_Pros______   **_Cons_**_____   ❏ *Looks good to me*

College (four-year liberal arts or specialized course of study in a college or university)

_Pros______   **_Cons_**_____   ❏ *Looks good to me*

Military service (full-time or ROTC)

_Pros______   **_Cons_**_____   ❏ *Looks good to me*

Work (any paying job or an internship in a profession of interest)

_Pros______   **_Cons_**_____   ❏ *Looks good to me*

Travel (seeing the world before making any big decisions)

_Pros______ **_Cons_**_____ ❏ **_Looks_**
good
_to me_

Volunteerism (unpaid position)

_Pros______ **_Cons_**_____ ❏ **_Looks_**
good
_to me_

Apprenticeship (formal on-the-job training to learn a specific trade)

_Pros______ **_Cons_**_____ ❏ **_Looks_**
good
_to me_

Other _____

_Pros______ **_Cons_**_____ ❏ **_Looks_**
good
_to me_

Two Heads Are Better Than One

Moses got it from his father-in-law Jethro. Samuel got it from his minister Eli. Timothy got it from his friend Paul. What was it? Good advice.

Scripture says it's a good thing to get. Especially when you're making big decisions. But finding guidance for tough decisions isn't the only benefit—check out these added perks.

Verses	Perks
Proverbs 2:1-12	[ ]
Proverbs 11:14	[ ]
Proverbs 15:22	[ ]
Proverbs 20:5	[ ]
Proverbs 27:9	[ ]

If You Were Me

Now that you're getting more ideas about what you might want to do with your life, it's time to tap into that wise counsel you just read about in Proverbs. Talk with at least three trusted adults: teacher, youth pastor, family friend, guidance counselor, parent. Tell them where you want to go with your life and the different ways you could get there. Then ask them the million-dollar question—

If you were me, what would you do? Write down their advice on the next page.

[Why Not You?]

Are you starstruck or plain ol' stuck? Sometimes our hopes and dreams are so big they can scare us to death. Fear of failure and lack of faith hold us back and keep us from even trying. Other times, being stuck is God's way of saying, "Hold on a minute, let's think this through a little bit more."

Here's an example. Suppose more than anything else in the world, you want to play basketball for the NBA. You've got the height, you've got the stats, you've got the scholarships. The opportunity is yours to win or lose. But c'mon, it's the NBA! It seems almost too good to be true. So what should you do? (Besides pray a lot and ask a lot of people for advice.)

How about going for it? Sure. It's your dream—go for it with all you've got. If it's meant to be, God will open doors all the way. If it's not and the door slams shut, another one will open down the road. Chances are it will be a door to an opportunity you'd never have discovered if you hadn't followed your dream.

On the other hand what if playing for the NBA is your dream, but you're only 5'10", you've got okay stats but you're no standout, and your allergies kick in every once in a while, making it hard to breathe. Reality check! However, basketball *is* your game. You live, eat, and sleep basketball. You watch all the games on TV; you cheer for the nearby professional team, the state college team, the local high school team, and your kid brother's YMCA team; and you're a virtual sports encyclopedia when it comes to all the pro teams, players, and coaches. You just can't see a future without basketball in it. So what should you do?

First, face the hard, cold fact that playing ball probably isn't going to pan out for you—although miracles do happen. Second, expand your horizons. *Playing* ball isn't the only way to enjoy the game. Take your strengths—energy, enthusiasm, knowledge of the game—and put them to work for you. How about becoming a sports journalist or college sports information director? What about sharing your love of the game with disadvantaged kids as a coach? There are lots of ways to blend your passion with your profession.

See for yourself. Pick an area you're really interested in, maybe business or the arts. Write that field of interest here.

Then pick the obvious profession for your area of interest. (For example, if your area of interest is business, then CEO of a corporation would be an obvious profession.) Write that obvious profession here.

Now think of as many other ways you could use that interest as you can and list them in the space that follows.

None of this is meant to imply you can't become an NBA superstar or head honcho of the next Microsoft. It's just meant to get you thinking of all the possibilities. Because somebody has to do each of those less obvious jobs. Why not you?

[The Good Life]

Success isn't all there is to life. Nope, God has lots more in store for you. Everything you need to have a good life. Read about it in the longest psalm—Psalm 119—and check which you supply and which God supplies.

Ingredients of a Good Life (verse number in parentheses)	God	Me
Blessings (1)	❑	❑
Dignity (6)	❑	❑
Purity (9)	❑	❑
Insight (18, 99)	❑	❑
Wise counsel (24)	❑	❑
Strength (28)	❑	❑
Freedom (32)	❑	❑
Salvation (41)	❑	❑
Comfort (52)	❑	❑
Thanksgiving (62)	❑	❑
Discernment (66)	❑	❑
Satisfaction (72)	❑	❑
Understanding (73)	❑	❑
Direction (105)	❑	❑
Joy (111)	❑	❑
Protection (114)	❑	❑
Rejoicing (162)	❑	❑
Peace (165)	❑	❑

What else could you possibly need? (Except maybe a vacation!)

[Christians at Work]

TOM MAHAIRAS
evangelist

Warning: This isn't the story of your typical goody-two-shoes preacher! The story starts out innocently enough, when Tom Mahairas was born in Thessalonika, Greece, and immigrated with his family to New York City as a young boy. But after years of struggling to master a new language and learn the ropes of a strange, new city, Tom found himself fully immersed in the hippie culture of the 1960s. He was a rebellious teenager at a time when rock 'n' roll, marijuana, free love, and the "if it feels good, do it" philosophy were big. Tom had a girlfriend, a rock band, and access to enough drugs to keep him out of his mind.

At one point—dazed and confused and wondering what life was all about—he ended up wandering around Central Park where someone told him he could find Jesus at a place called Word of Life Island. Desperate enough to try anything, Tom hitchhiked upstate to Word of Life's Christian camp facility and started looking for Jesus—literally *looking* for Jesus, which should give you a pretty good idea of his state of mind at the time. And two days later Tom found him—not in the way he'd expected, of course, but through a young man who shared the truth of John 3:16 with him. Tom accepted Christ right then and there as the truth he'd been searching for and immediately called his girlfriend Vicky to share what he'd found with her.

These transformed hippies—Tom and Vicky—enrolled in one of the most conservative Christian colleges in the world and prepared for a life of serving God. After graduating in 1971 they married, returned to New York City, and started holding Bible studies in their apartment. These Bible studies eventually grew into what is now the Manhattan Bible Church—a ministry that includes a church, a Christian school, and a variety of outreach programs.

In 1996 Tom felt God leading him into a new ministry. An evangelist at heart, Tom turned over the pastorate of the church and started Citivision, an organization devoted to local and international evangelism as well as equipping urban pastors and churches with the tools to reach their communities. Tom now travels all over the world helping Christians make God real to unsaved and unchurched people. Tom's work also involves discipleship, hands-on training, church planting, and oversight of a variety of ministries, all allowing him to use his God-given gifts with people who need to find Jesus.

Whether it's through a bowl of hot soup for a homeless person, job training for a single parent, or a spiritual retreat for a burned-out pastor, there are many ways to help people find Jesus—and Tom has devoted his life to doing just that.

To find out more about Tom's ministry, visit his Web site at www.citivision.org.

[Up and At 'Em]

Guess how many different careers there are for you to choose from? If you're like most people, you can probably think of about 25 ideas. That's a nice start, but the experts who use your parents' hard-earned tax dollars to keep track of these things say there are actually more than 20,000 different ways Americans earn a living every day. Big difference, huh?

Maybe you've never even heard of the job that's the best one for you. Maybe it hasn't even been invented yet! That's why it's so important to get out and see what's up. Check it out—*it* being your options, your choices, your future. You didn't think someone was going to hand you a road map for getting where you want to go in life, did you? Sorry. No *Yahoo!* maps here.

Let's get started!

[Mind Expansion]

Chances are you know about more jobs than you give yourself credit for. Take this little test and see. First, take this journal and head for your favorite hangout—the mall, burger joint, bookstore, music store—whatever. Write that place here.

[If you're completing this journal with your youth group, your youth pastor may organize activities to help you complete the activities in this section. If not, gather a couple friends and do them on your own.]

Think of all the jobs it takes to make that favorite place of yours happen. If it involves food, start at the beginning—from the farmer all the way to the guy behind the counter—and list all the people it takes to keep that food coming. Same thing with clothes—start with the raw materials and work your way through to the finished products hanging in the store.

You'll be amazed at all the opportunities you discover. Don't stop until your list is complete!

1.	23.
2.	24.
3.	25.
4.	26.
5.	27.
6.	28.
7.	29.
8.	30.
9.	31.
10.	32.
11.	33.
12.	34.
13.	35.
14.	36.
15.	37.
16.	38.
17.	39.
18.	40.
19.	41.
20.	42.
21.	43.
22.	44.

45.   73.
46.   74.
47.   75.
48.   76.
49.   77.
50.   78.
51.   79.
52.   80.
53.   81.
54.   82.
55.   83.
56.   84.
57.   85.
58.   86.
59.   87.
60.   88.
61.   89.
62.   90.
63.   91.
64.   92.
65.   93.
66.   94.
67.   95.
68.   96.
69.   97.
70.   98.
71.   99.
72.   100.

[Get Thee to a Library!]

Pick a career you want to know more about and write it here—

Now explore the library or the resources available to find out more about your chosen profession. The resources mentioned on pages 46-47 will help you.

So what about that career you've researched...

1. What do people working in this profession do all day?

2. What kinds of skills do they use on the job?

3. What education and training do they need?

4. What kinds of employers hire people to do this kind of work? List names of companies if you find them.

5. How much money does a person make in this profession when starting out?

6. What opportunities are available for people in this profession as they gain more experience and training?

7. How much demand is expected for this type of worker in the next 10 years or so?

8. What careers are similar to this one that require less training? That require more training?

9. What abilities and interests do you have that might make a career like this a good fit for you?

10. How would a job like this allow you to honor God with your work?

Is this career for you?

❏ Yes! This is it! I'm going to trust God to open doors and see where it takes me.
❏ No! Anything but this!
❏ Maybe. This one sounds interesting, but I need more information before I decide.

[Check It Out]

It's so obvious. You need information. The library *has* information. Get the two of you together, and you'll have the knowledge to start making an informed decision about your future!

Get Thee to a Library!

- Check out the books with call numbers 331.702—this is where you'll find general information about all kinds of careers. A great place to start the search.
- Check out the reference section with call numbers 331.702—sometimes the best stuff is in this section. You can't check these books out, so bring some change to pay for copies of information you want to keep.
- Check under specific topics such as engineering or healthcare when you want to get more in-depth about a specific profession.

And You Won't Want to Miss...

The Adams Job Almanac *edited by Adam Graber (Adams Media Corp., 1999)*

America's Top 300 Jobs *edited by J. Michael Farr (Jist Books, 2000)*

Cool Careers for Dummies *by Marty Nemko with Paul and Sarah Edwards (1998)*

100 Best Careers for the 21st Century *by Shelly Field (2000)*

100 Jobs in the Environment *by Debra Quintana (1997)*

100 Jobs in Social Change *by Harley Jebens (1997)*

100 Jobs in Technology *by Lori Hawkins and Betsy Dowling* (1997)

100 Jobs in Words *by Scott A. Meyer* (1997)

—all published by IDG Books Worldwide

The following books contain excellent information on careers, although they're written for slightly younger readers.

Career Ideas for Kids Who Like Animals & Nature (2000)

Career Ideas for Kids Who Like Art (1998)

Career Ideas for Kids Who Like Computers (1998)

Career Ideas for Kids Who Like Math (2000)

Career Ideas for Kids Who Like Science (1998)

Career Ideas for Kids Who Like Sports (1998)

Career Ideas for Kids Who Like Talking (1998)

Career Ideas for Kids Who Like Writing (1998)

—all by Diane Lindsey Reeves (Checkmark Books)

Cool Careers for Girls in Air & Space (2000)

Cool Careers for Girls in Computers (1999)

Cool Careers for Girls in Construction (2000)

Cool Careers for Girls in Engineering (1999)

Cool Careers for Girls in Food (1999)

Cool Careers for Girls in Health (1999)

Cool Careers for Girls in Law (2000)

Cool Careers for Girls in Performing Arts (2000)

Cool Careers for Girls in Sports (1999)

Cool Careers for Girls with Animals (1999)

—all by Ceel Pasternak and Linda Thornburg (Impact Publishing)

[Surf's Up!]

Lucky you. You're the first generation to have access to the wonders of the Internet. Anything you could possibly want to know—about nearly anything—you can find with a few clicks. Try it. Career information, college applications, job-hunting—it's all there!

So pick a career—any career that might interest you—and see whether you can find the following information. Write down the exact Web site address for each site you visit and print out pages with information you want to keep.

The profession—

Profile of the profession—

College or training program to get prepared for this career—

Professional associations—

Employers who hire people in this profession—

Hot trends or current projects in this profession—

Here are some sites you may want to visit—

careerideasforkids.com   careermag.com
careermosaic.com   careerpathsonline.com
careerplanning.about.com   futurescan.com
ivillage.com/career   review.com

[The Family Business]

If you're completing this journal with your youth group, your church may host Grabbing Tried and True Tips from Familiar Faces where you can talk to adults from your church about their work. If not, check with your school guidance counselor to find out about career fairs and events in your town. Many high schools, colleges, and community organizations conduct career fairs every year. Use the space below to record information about the people you meet and the jobs they enjoy.

[Little Black Book]

The little black book—an important tool of successful people everywhere. These days it may be in an electronic organizer or on a computer. Wherever, you need a place to keep track of people you meet and information you receive from them. And you may keep your goals, calendar, and some wishful thinking there, too!

Here's your chance to get one started.

Job leads—

Places I'd like to work someday—

People I'd like to work with someday—

Ministries I'd like to serve in someday—

[Next Steps]

You've covered a lot of ground. So what's next? It depends on where you are. Maybe by now you know exactly how you want to launch the next stage of your life. Maybe you're more confused than ever and worried you'll never figure it all out.

Well, you'll know you're on the right track if these road signs all point in the same direction—

- The Bible
- Common sense
- Personal desire
- Wise counsel
- Answered prayers
- Circumstances
- Inner impressions (peace)

Consider taking a career inventory like the Self-Directed Search [Psychological Assessment Resources Inc.]. Ask your school counselor [you may not have to pay a charge if you take it through your school] or look on the Internet at www.self-directed-search.com [where it costs less than $10].

Maybe you've got mixed signals and aren't totally sure what to do, but you've narrowed your options.

If you're freaking out about ever finding your future, take heart. You're already much further ahead than most people your age. At least you're thinking about the possibilities, checking out options, asking for help, and seeking God's guidance.

If you know where you're headed, what do you need to do next to keep things moving in the right direction? Look at colleges to get the training you need? Improve your grades so you can get into college? Talk with more people in the profession to get their advice?

If you're not sure, what do you need to do to find out more? To explore more options? To get more help?

Either way, make a checklist here. Star one idea you can do in the next 24 hours—and do it!

❑ _____   ❑ _____

❑ _____   ❑ _____

❑ _____   ❑ _____

❑ _____   ❑ _____

❑ _____   ❑ _____

Don't stop now. You've learned important skills to help you make an informed decision. So keep praying. Keep talking with people. Keep searching out answers. You'll figure it out—just in the nick of time.

[It's All Yours, God]

All you are, all you ever hope to be—all by the grace of God. Use the space below to write a prayer giving everything over to him. Give him all your hopes and dreams, all your fears and frustrations, all your failures and successes. Commit yourself to "trust and obey" (in the words of an old hymn). Ask him to guide you each step of the way. Thank him for his promises and faithfulness.

Resources from YOUTH SPECIALTIES

Youth Ministry Programming

Camps, Retreats, Missions, & Service Ideas (Ideas Library)

Compassionate Kids: Practical Ways to Involve Your Students in Mission and Service

Creative Bible Lessons from the Old Testament

Creative Bible Lessons in 1 & 2 Corinthians

Creative Bible Lessons in John: Encounters with Jesus

Creative Bible Lessons in Romans: Faith on Fire!

Creative Bible Lessons on the Life of Christ

Creative Bible Lessons in Psalms

Creative Junior High Programs from A to Z, Vol. 1 (A-M)

Creative Junior High Programs from A to Z, Vol. 2 (N-Z)

Creative Meetings, Bible Lessons, & Worship Ideas (Ideas Library)

Crowd Breakers & Mixers (Ideas Library)

Downloading the Bible Leader's Guide

Drama, Skits, & Sketches (Ideas Library)

Drama, Skits, & Sketches 2 (Ideas Library)

Dramatic Pauses

Everyday Object Lessons

Games (Ideas Library)

Games 2 (Ideas Library)

Good Sex: A Whole-Person Approach to Teenage Sexuality & God

Great Fundraising Ideas for Youth Groups

More Great Fundraising Ideas for Youth Groups

Great Retreats for Youth Groups

Holiday Ideas (Ideas Library)

Hot Illustrations for Youth Talks

More Hot Illustrations for Youth Talks

Still More Hot Illustrations for Youth Talks

Ideas Library on CD-ROM

Incredible Questionnaires for Youth Ministry

Junior High Game Nights

More Junior High Game Nights

Kickstarters: 101 Ingenious Intros to Just about Any Bible Lesson

Live the Life! Student Evangelism Training Kit

Memory Makers

The Next Level Leader's Guide

Play It! Over 150 Great Games for Youth Groups

Roaring Lambs

So What Am I Gonna Do with My Life? Leader's Guide

Special Events (Ideas Library)

Spontaneous Melodramas

Spontaneous Melodramas 2

Student Leadership Training Manual

Student Underground: An Event Curriculum on the Persecuted Church

Super Sketches for Youth Ministry

Talking the Walk

Videos That Teach

What Would Jesus Do? Youth Leader's Kit

Wild Truth Bible Lessons

Wild Truth Bible Lessons 2

Wild Truth Bible Lessons—Pictures of God

Wild Truth Bible Lessons—Pictures of God 2

Worship Services for Youth Groups

Professional Resources

Administration, Publicity, & Fundraising (Ideas Library)

Dynamic Communicators Workshop for Youth Workers

Equipped to Serve: Volunteer Youth Worker Training Course

Help! I'm a Junior High Youth Worker!

Help! I'm a Small-Group Leader!

Help! I'm a Sunday School Teacher!

Help! I'm a Volunteer Youth Worker!

How to Expand Your Youth Ministry

How to Speak to Youth...and Keep Them Awake at the Same Time

Junior High Ministry (Updated & Expanded)

The Ministry of Nurture: A Youth Worker's Guide to Discipling Teenagers

Postmodern Youth Ministry

Purpose-Driven Youth Ministry

Purpose-Driven Youth Ministry Training Kit

So *That's* Why I Keep Doing This! 52 Devotional Stories for Youth Workers

Teaching the Bible Creatively
A Youth Ministry Crash Course
Youth Ministry Management Tools
The Youth Worker's Handbook to Family Ministry

Academic Resources

Four Views of Youth Ministry and the Church
Starting Right: Thinking Theologically about Youth
    Ministry

Discussion Starters

Discussion & Lesson Starters (Ideas Library)
Discussion & Lesson Starters 2 (Ideas Library)
EdgeTV
Get 'Em Talking
Keep 'Em Talking!
Good Sex: A Whole-Person Approach to Teenage
    Sexuality & God
High School TalkSheets
More High School TalkSheets
High School TalkSheets from Psalms and Proverbs
Junior High TalkSheets
More Junior High TalkSheets
Junior High TalkSheets from Psalms and Proverbs
Real Kids: Short Cuts
Real Kids: The Real Deal—on Friendship, Loneliness,
    Racism, & Suicide
Real Kids: The Real Deal—on Sexual Choices, Family
    Matters, & Loss
Real Kids: The Real Deal—on Stressing Out,
    Addictive Behavior, Great Comebacks, & Violence
Real Kids: Word on the Street
Unfinished Sentences: 450 Tantalizing Statement-
    Starters to Get Teenagers Talking & Thinking
What If...? 450 Thought-Provoking Questions to Get
    Teenagers Talking, Laughing, and Thinking
Would You Rather...? 465 Provocative Questions to Get
    Teenagers Talking
Have You Ever...? 450 Intriguing Questions
    Guaranteed to Get Teenagers Talking

Art Source Clip Art

Stark Raving Clip Art (print)
Youth Group Activities (print)
Clip Art Library Version 2.0 (CD-ROM)

Digital Resources

Clip Art Library Version 2.0 (CD-ROM)
Ideas Library on CD-ROM
Youth Ministry Management Tools (CD-ROM)

Videos & Video Curricula

Dynamic Communicators Workshop for Youth Workers
EdgeTV
Equipped to Serve: Volunteer Youth Worker Training
    Course
Good Sex: A Whole-Person Approach to Teenage
    Sexuality & God
The Heart of Youth Ministry: A Morning with Mike
    Yaconelli
Live the Life! Student Evangelism Training Kit
Purpose-Driven Youth Ministry Training Kit
Real Kids: Short Cuts
Real Kids: The Real Deal—on Friendship, Loneliness,
    Racism, & Suicide
Real Kids: The Real Deal—on Sexual Choices, Family
    Matters, & Loss
Real Kids: The Real Deal—on Stressing Out,
    Addictive Behavior, Great Comebacks, & Violence
Real Kids: Word on the Street
Student Underground: An Event Curriculum on the
    Persecuted Church
Understanding Your Teenager Video Curriculum

Student Resources

Downloading the Bible: A Rough Guide to the New
    Testament
Downloading the Bible: A Rough Guide to the Old
    Testament
Grow For It Journal
Grow For It Journal through the Scriptures
So What Am I Gonna Do with My Life? Journaling
    Workbook for Students
Spiritual Challenge Journal: The Next Level
Teen Devotional Bible
What Almost Nobody Will Tell You about Sex
What Would Jesus Do? Spiritual Challenge Journal
Wild Truth Journal for Junior Highers
Wild Truth Journal—Pictures of God